Femvertising and Empowerment

Can advertising ever facilitate the empowerment of women?

Lisa-Marie Koller

MA Advertising Strategy & Planning

Falmouth University

18.07.2018

This report was submitted in partial fulfillment of the requirements of the award of MA Advertising Strategy & Planning. I, Lisa-Marie Koller, confirm that, except where other sources are acknowledged, this project is my own unaided work and that its length is 7671 words.

Date......18.07.2018
Cover Photo by Lisa-Marie Koller

Representation
is vital
otherwise the butterfly
surrounded by a group of moths
unable to see itself
will keep trying to become the moth

representation – rupi kaur

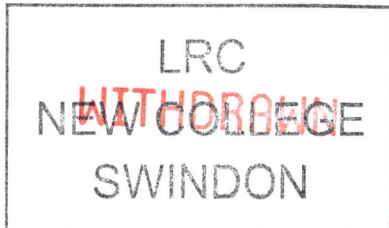

Table of contents

1. Introduction

As a result of an increasing awareness of the ongoing inequality, mistreatment and misrepresentation of women in society, recently, a number of social media and celebrity driven protest movements have emerged. These campaign-like advances are spear headed by two prominent movements against sexual harassment or assault on women, namely '#MeToo' and '#TimesUp', which aim to empower women by giving them the tools to make themselves heard, as well as creating a community full of support and encouragement for other women who are in similar situations (cf. MeToo 2018 and Time's Up Now 2017).

In the advertising industry, the newfound awareness of these feminist issues has resulted in the formation of a new trend often referred to as 'femvertising'. In this trend, brands and agencies have started to employ feminist language (e.g. 'empowerment') and agenda in their branding and ads in order to, seemingly, bring positive social change. This trend, further, seems to bring an end to the age-old discussion of whether advertising merely 'mirrors' society or 'shapes' it as well. While it has been found that advertising, historically, typically mirrored society rather than actively challenged the predominant female stereotypes and roles (Eisend 2010), it is a mistake to conclude that advertising does not shape society at the same time. In fact, by reinforcing the same stereotypes or discourses time and again, ads desensitize their audience to certain ideologies and, in consequence, contribute to shaping society (Blloshmi 2013). The part that advertising plays in the contribution to changes in societal discourses is especially valuable nowadays, as consumers are susceptible to advertising almost anywhere (most prominently on their smart phones but also on TV, outdoor billboards etc.) and anytime, even unconsciously (cf. Story 2007 and Forer 2018). Due to the potential negative effects this can have, especially regarding the perpetuation of harmful stereotypes, the ASA has issued a report on gender stereotypes which "provides an evidence-based case for stronger regulation of ads that feature stereotypical gender roles or characteristics which might be harmful to people, including ads which mock people for not conforming to gender stereotypes" (ASA and CAP 2018, also cf. ASA 2017). As advertisers have recognized this potential of adverts to bring positive change upon society, in combination with the aforementioned rise of awareness of 'feminist issues', 'femvertising' has come to the foreground. These ads cater to a new kind of consumer, while seemingly furthering the breaking down of stereotypes and misrepresentation, as well as contributing to the eventual equality of women and men. However, there has been some criticism from feminist scholars, such as Andi Zeisler, who claim that advertising can never really empower women in the true sense of the word. Additionally, the bottom-line purpose of ads is to sell a product or image and, therefore, is exploiting the movement.

This work aims to investigate the notion of empowerment in advertising and explore femvertising through the lived experiences of several women in order to try to answer the question "Can ads genuinely facilitate the empowerment of women?" and, consequently, "How?".

For that purpose, in the first part of the project, the concept of empowerment in the context of advertising will be reviewed critically to arrive at the hypothesis that advertising has the potential to contribute to the empowerment of women, despite being accused of appropriating feminism through 'false empowerment', i.e. using this kind of mainstream capitalist version of empowerment to avoid real empowerment and equality. The second part comprises a small-scale research project that includes the analysis of individual in-depth interviews with six women. As part of the interviews, the women were asked to compare and contrast two representative 'femvertising' ads ('#LikeAGirl' by *Always* and '#StressTest' by *Secret*) that were chosen carefully in order to examine their attitudes towards advertising campaigns that claim to empower women. Out of this analysis, certain themes emerged that help to strengthen the hypothesis, as well as answer the research questions.

2. The empowerment of women in advertising

In order to be able to adequately tackle the complex issue of women's empowerment through advertising the many and varied meanings of 'empowerment' need to be defined and contextualized. Empowerment in its classic form of giving voice to those with less power is an issue for any section of society that is silenced by virtue of class, race, ability and sexuality. The focus of this project is to look specifically at the empowered or disempowered voice of women as represented by mainstream advertising as this is one of the major vehicles that contribute to shaping social norms. Therefore, this section will discuss different aspects of empowerment in terms of power relations between men and women. This will then be explored and critiqued through the recent trend of 'femvertising'.

2.1 Empowerment in a patriarchal system

The question 'What is empowerment?' can partly be answered by briefly reiterating the origin of the need for such a concept and why it is still relevant today. The unlimited and unconditional equality of women and men is an issue that is at the heart of feminism (cf. Griffin 2017); it has been fought for by women (and men) for decades. While power structures may have shifted somewhat over the years (women have gained the right to vote and are even free to pursue whichever career they want to), the need for feminism and empowerment is still alive and well today (cf. Zeisler 2016 and Penny 2017). The gender pay gap, laws restricting women's rights regarding their own bodies (e.g. abortion laws in the US) and an evident lack of women in leading positions are just some of the issues that can be observed. Stigmas and stereotypes deeply rooted in our cultures still exist to hold these structures in place. These thought patterns are not only blatantly present in influential media forms, such as TV and advertising, but also in science (cf. Saini 2017).

As science is a field that is trusted by most people to deliver objective facts, free from prejudice, it influences our way of thinking and living. Addressing the inequality of women, Saini puts it this way, "For centuries, scientists have influenced decision-makers on important issues including abortion rights, granting women the vote, and how schools educate us. They have shaped how we think about our minds and bodies, and our relationships with each other" (2017: 1). However, an acknowledged problem within the scientific community is unconscious bias. It can influence scientists' ways of setting up projects, phrasing questions or even interpreting the outcome of a study. Following this, it can be concluded that, by impacting each other, science, politics and various media forms (including advertising) create a vicious circle that perpetuates stereotypes in our society. This is where empowerment comes into play. It is an important tool to help break this circle.

In short, the Oxford Dictionary of Gender Studies defines empowerment as "a concept that refers to the giving or delegation of authority to someone to enable them to deal on their own or others' behalf" (Griffin 2017). This definition of empowerment, however, can be considered problematic. It involves someone (most likely a man) 'in power' giving up part of their power, seemingly 'allowing' a woman to make her own decisions and, therefore, by extension, staying in power. This correlates to Mary Beard's view on the need for a different way of thinking about power. She argues that if power is treated as "an object of possession that only the few – mostly men – can own or wield [...] women as a gender – not as some individuals – are by definition excluded from it" (Beard 2017: 86). Beard urges the reader to think about power differently, as something collaborative and active, in order to make a difference and change the structure. According to her, "It is power in that sense that many women feel they don't have – and that they want" (Beard 2017: 87). The existing predominance of the male 'voice' can also be observed in the world of advertising. Although women control 64 percent of a household's income (Onuoha 2016), less than 25 percent of creative or design roles in UK advertising agencies (with the number declining even further in decision making positions) are occupied by women (Usborne 2016).

Considering the different aspects of empowerment presented so far, it becomes apparent that agency is a key element of empowerment. However, in this context, Huis et al. point out that merely the ability of women to choose for themselves will not necessarily result in any structural changes, as "women's individual choices are historically and structurally conditioned" (2017: 2). Therefore, empowerment, as well as agency, must be considered in a more inclusive way. Huis et al. define empowerment as a "multifaceted process, which involves individual as well as collective awareness, beliefs, and behavior embedded in the social structure of specific cultural contexts" (2017: 3). From this it can be concluded that empowerment is a complex multi-layered process that cannot merely be granted to individuals or a group, i.e. women, by someone from outside. Consequently, the answer to the question 'Can ads genuinely facilitate the empowerment of women?' cannot be an absolute 'yes'. Hence, there is a need to further investigate how exactly empowerment can be facilitated and if advertising could potentially contribute to this.

In her report *Women's Empowerment: What Works?*, Andrea Cornwall suggests that there are a few ways in which external actors can contribute to empowerment:

> Clearing obstacles from commonly travelled paths; supporting stopping places for women to gather to reflect on their journeys and gain tips, route-maps, courage and the company of others; providing signposts, stiles, bridges and sustenance for those making these journeys. (2016: 345)

She goes on by stating that, however, in order to address the "deep structural basis of gender inequality" more than this is needed:

> Two vital levers are needed. The first is processes that produce *shifts in consciousness* [original emphasis]. This includes overturning limiting normative beliefs and expectations that keep women locked into situations of subordination and dependency, challenging restrictive cultural and social norms and contesting the institutions of everyday life that sustain inequity. [...] The second is engagement with culturally embedded normative beliefs, understandings and ideas about gender, power and change. (2016: 345)

Considering Cornwall's approach in the context of advertising, it becomes clear that ads do not have the potential to 'genuinely facilitate' but to 'contribute to' the empowerment of women. While it is often argued that advertisements merely mirror discourses which are already existent in society (cf. Eisend 2010), it has been established that this is not the case (cf. ASA 2017, Unilever 2017b, Blloshmi 2013). In fact, advertising selectively mirrors only certain parts of society and, by that, contributes to shaping it at the same time. By continuously reinforcing the same dominant discourses, ads "desensitize audiences to these subliminal ideologies therefore neutralizing opposition to them" (Blloshmi 2013: 23). As a logical consequence, this potential of shaping discourses within society should be viewed as an opportunity to contribute to the empowerment of women. Cornwall mentioned 'overturning limiting normative beliefs and expectations' and engagement with these as a way towards empowerment (see above). This could potentially be done through advertising by including all kinds of aspects that differentiate women. This includes the mere representation of different body types, skin colors, professions, ages or hobbies, as well as telling stories from women's perspectives. As Cornwall states, "Changing these representations is a form of social action that can have a powerful impact on women's sense of their own power" (2016: 354). Additionally, this issue is something that consumers nowadays are already aware of. Not only do many women feel misrepresented by advertising, but also 91% believe that how women are portrayed in ads has a direct impact on girls' self-esteem (Skey 2015). Furthermore, in addition to an adequate representation of women, addressing these issues in ads could potentially foster an awareness among girls and women which could then result in a shift in consciousness. In that way, advertising could be used as a force for positive social change. Out of this last point, recently, a heavily criticized trend often referred to as 'femvertising' has emerged. This trend and the criticism it has attracted will be discussed in the following section.

2.2 The emergence of 'femvertising'

The term 'femvertising' was coined by SheKnowsMedia, the founders of the femvertising awards, as part of a study on this topic conducted by them in 2014. They define femvertising as "advertising that employs pro-female talent, messages, and imagery to empower women and girls" (Skey 2015). Yet, the early beginnings of femvertising can be traced back to 2004 when Dove launched their 'Campaign for Real Beauty' or, arguably, even further back into the 1970s where the first Nike adverts employed a language of feminism and empowerment to challenge gender stereotypes (cf. Unilever 2017a and EMGN 2017). In this context, the term can also be defined, more academically, as "advertising that challenges traditional female advertising stereotypes" (Akestam et al. 2017: 796).

In recent years femvertising has seen a surge in ads that were celebrated among the advertising industry and consumers alike. These include popular TV spots that were widely shared on social media via YouTube, for example, '#LikeAGirl' by *Always*, 'This girl can' by *Sport England*,

'Imagine the Possibilities' by *Barbie* and 'Daughter' by *Audi* (cf. Nudd 2017). Most of these ads target women and mainly address issues of gender stereotypes in combination with a plea for women to feel empowered by certain things, such as their bodies or the right (self-care) product.

In that way, 'This girl can', for example, seems to send out the message that women should feel empowered by their own body, no matter their shape or size, as long as they are leading an active lifestyle. Additionally, the *Barbie* spot seems to portray the idea that it is still unimaginable for women to have leading positions in society. Yet, with the help of the right product, namely a *Barbie* doll (that still perpetuates unrealistic body standards), girls will be empowered by having the tools to imagine they can be everything they want.

Arguably, the odd one out here is 'Daughter' by *Audi*. It not only targets women and men, but also features a girl that wins a race full of boys merely because of her skills. This suggests that women or girls can be empowered through their abilities. Furthermore, the spot addresses an important political issue of gender inequality, the gender pay gap.

In June 2017, the trend of femvertising saw its figurative culmination (to date) in the launch of the

Unstereotype Alliance in Cannes. It is a "new global Alliance set to banish stereotypical portrayals of gender in advertising and all brand led content" that was founded by "UN Women in partnership with Unilever and industry leaders including WPP, IPG, facebook, Google, Mars, Microsoft and J&J" (Unilever 2017b). Although this initiative, as well as femvertising in general, are celebrated by many (by some it is even referred to as a gateway to feminism (cf. Pankhurst 2018)), the trend is also criticized heavily. To lay part of the basis for the analysis to follow in section 4, the two main arguments raised by critics of the trend will be dissected in the remaining part of this section.

One of the main arguments presented against femvertising emerged from the ranks of feminist scholars and advocates, such as Angela McRobbie (2009) and Andi Zeisler (2016). It positions femvertising as part of a discourse which appropriates feminism in order to mask political or 'real' issues of inequality, such as the gender pay gap, women's right of bodily autonomy (regarding laws against abortion, for example), the major absence of women in leadership positions and even violence against women. Here, it has to be noted that this is, obviously, not an exhaustive list of issues of gender inequality, especially when various cultures around the world are taken into consideration. Yet, to date, they are the most visible in our 'Western' culture. Different scholars pursue different ways of approaching this discourse; it might be referred to as 'commodity feminism' (Dowsett 2010), 'hegemonic feminism' (Eisenstein 2017), 'confidence culture' (Gill and Orgad 2017), 'post-feminist spectatorship' (Calkin 2015) or 'market place feminism' (Zeisler 2016). However, they all point to the same argument: Femvertising aims to mask true issues of inequality and avoid structural changes. Instead, by feigning empowerment, it calls upon women individually and collectively to change themselves and their bodies in order to have a shot at equality.

One way in which this is done is by employing the idea that "female consumers are empowered by their personal consumer choices" (Zeisler 2016: 18). Yet, this is not a new strategy. It was already, famously, implemented by Philip Morris in the 1970s. The cigarette company launched a campaign for their new brand for women 'Virginia Slims' with the tagline 'You've come a long way, baby'. Additionally, cigarettes were branded as 'torches of freedom' (Bernays 1965) suggesting that having the choice of whether or not to smoke and, in extension, which cigarette brand to buy results in a great accomplishment for equality and, additionally, empowerment. Yet, McRobbie suggests that feminism is made to seem redundant by focusing on these tropes of freedom and choice (2009). She even argues that "women are currently being disempowered through the very discourses of empowerment they are being offered as substitutes for feminism" (2009: 49). In line with this statement, Zeisler maintains that empowerment has become

> a way to signify a particularly female way of being that's both gender-essentialist [...] and commercially motivated [...] [including] High heels. Flats. Cosmetic surgery. Embracing your wrinkles. Having children. Not having children [etc.] (2016: 169).

Empowerment was even referred to as merely "the ability to do what you want to do" by a tabloid magazine (Zeisler 2016: 170). Furthermore, Calkin argues that within this discourse, women's empowerment is only desirable "to the extent that it generates overall economic growth" (2015: 663).

Another aspect that contributes to the criticism of femvertising is the notion that to overcome any problem which is rooted in gender inequality, women should change their behavior. The main focus here lies on female self-confidence. According to Gill and Orgad, women are made to realize that they are being held back by their own individual lack of confidence, which is not connected to any structural inequalities, institutionalized sexism or cultural forces (2017). They argue that,

16

these circulating discourses of self-love and self-confidence constitute [...] a move deeper into women's psyches so that women must work not just on developing a [sic] 'a beautiful body' but also 'a beautiful mind' – an 'upgraded' form of selfhood in which there is no space for vulnerability or ambivalence, but only for compulsory body love and self-confidence. (Gill and Orgad 2017: 26)

Following this argument, femvertising encourages women to change their individual behavior or appearance under the pretext of feminism and, more specifically, empowerment. This ties in with Zeisler's view on market place feminism. She states that market place feminism gives women the impression that if they hit walls in any part of their life, it has nothing to do with gender "but with problems that can be resolved with better self-esteem, more confidence, maybe some life coaching" (Zeisler 2016: 255). Moreover, as part of her book *We were feminists once* she examines some femvertising campaigns, including *Dove's* 'Real Beauty' and *Cover Girl's* '#GirlsCan' campaign, citing them as examples of how brands are telling girls and women that they can be whatever they want but at the same time selling them a product that is linked to achieving this, i.e. a body lotion made to smooth out cellulite or any other beauty product. This already touches upon the second main argument against femvertising: the brand's agenda or the true purpose of the ads which is to generate profit.

The main point that is raised in this argument is the fact that an ad's true purpose is, ultimately, always to sell a product or to change consumers' perception of a brand. This goes directly against the agenda of feminism. As Penny puts it, "feminism is about putting more power in the hands of women, not putting more profit in the pockets of [...] companies" (2017: 230). Yet, through femvertising, feminism and especially empowerment are used to do just that. Unilever is one of the big companies that is often referenced as an example to underline this argument. In particular, they are criticized for the conflicting messages they are conveying while also perpetuating certain gender stereotypes. By making use of their brand *Dove*, for example, "Unilever sells women 'empowerment' in the global North with the message that different sizes and colors of bodies are beautiful [while, at the same time, selling] skin lightening cream in the global South [saying] that lighter-colored skin is more beautiful and desirable" (Dowsett 2010: 3). Furthermore, it is regularly pointed out that Unilever also owns brands, such as *Lynx* (or *Axe* outside the UK) the products of which are advertised using sexism and body fascism (Penny 2017: 175).

The aim of this section was to provide a basis for the analysis of two representative femvertising ads, by defining empowerment and the possibilities of its facilitation, followed by a discussion of the recent femvertising trend and the criticism that comes with it.

This work explores femvertising, through a small-scale research project, into the lived experiences of several women and their views on femvertising and the associated empowerment messages contained within femvertising. The aim and objectives are as follows:

Aim:

- Examine female attitudes towards advertising campaigns claimed to empower women, which are of value in the process of comprehensively answering the question 'Can ads genuinely facilitate the empowerment of women?' and, consequently, 'How?'

Objectives:

- Identify two recent and representative contemporary 'femvertising' campaigns for analysis of advertising message and narrative
- Investigate attitudes and perceptions of women towards body care products

- Investigate attitudes and perceptions of women towards femvertising, through in-depth interviews focused on the selected advertising campaigns

3. The Methodology

In addition to a literature review, the methodology that was applied in order to answer the research question is qualitative in-depth interviews. This approach was chosen instead of a focus group or a quantitative survey as it fits well within the frame of feminist research and empowerment (cf. Cornwall 2016). It is important to consider the individual voices of women and record their responses to get a plurality of voices and an idea of what is important to them and moves them. Furthermore, one-to-one interviews allow the respondents to take their time to process their thoughts and be able to articulate what they would like to say without being influenced by others. Additionally, this setting allows for the creation of a safe space in which respondents can express their emotions freely. All of this is crucial in getting to the bottom of their reception of femvertising ads and, further, to answer the research question.

For the analysis, the ads that were shown to the interviewees are '#LikeAGirl' for *Always* (directed by

Lauren Greenfield for Leo Burnett, launched Jan. 29 2015) and two short clips of the '#StressTest'-campaign for *Secret* (created by Wieden+Kennedy, launched April 11 2016). These ads were chosen for several reasons. First, the two campaigns are representative of the femvertising trend as they employ the issue of women's empowerment as their main advertising strategy. Furthermore, they are both adverts for body care products, i.e. maxi pads and deodorant. This is also representative of the trend as most femvertising ads were made for products that, in some way, regulate and compensate for the female body (cf. McRobbie 2009 and de Waal Malefyt and McCabe 2016). However, the two chosen adverts also show a few differences that allow for comparison and contrast in the analysis. Among adverts or campaigns such as 'Real Beauty' by *Dove*, 'Better for it' or 'Unlimited You' by *Nike*, 'Imagine the Possibilities' by *Barbie* and 'This girl can' by *Sport England*, '#LikeAGirl' is part of a few of the most widely shared and celebrated ads claiming to empower women (cf. D&AD 2018, Foote 2016, Google 2016, Nudd 2017 and oneupweb 2017). In contrast, the '#StressTest'-campaign has not resonated with such a big audience. Another difference between the ads, and most likely part of the reason for the difference in reception, is the execution. While '#LikeAGirl' is a 3:18 minutes long emotional video which could almost be described as an 'epic' among ads and that is designed to stay on top of the consumer's mind for a long time, the '#StressTest' campaign consists of a few short light-hearted videos that do not have the same effect. Furthermore, there is a difference in what the ads are seemingly advertising. '#LikeAGirl' is not recognizably tied to a certain product but is promoting the brand image. The '#StressTest' campaign, however, clearly shows the product that is advertised at the end of each video and puts it in context with the message. In addition, and arguably most importantly for the purpose of this project, the empowerment of women is realized in a different way in both ads. This last point will be the main focus of the analysis.

The women that were chosen as participants were selected according to three criteria: professional background, age and nationality. These criteria, reflect the participants' social/educational status, generation and the culture they were brought up in. Consequently, the respondents include women from different cultures (Austria, Germany, Slovenia, France and Turkey), age groups (25-48) and with different professional backgrounds (from entry level to leading positions in the fields of translation, marketing, business management, as well as food technology and science). This selection allows for a consideration of responses from European participants with diverse backgrounds and views of life, which is crucial for the attempt of finding a representative answer to the research question.

Informed consent and ethical considerations

All six interviews were recorded to provide detailed data. The recordings were then analyzed and transcribed for salient points relating to the research questions. Throughout, the participants' identity is protected by anonymizing their data to guarantee their privacy. Please see Appendix 1 for a copy of the informed consent form for this project, read and signed by all participants prior to the interview.

In addition to issues of consent and confidentiality, integrity and trust are part of ethical considerations that have to be taken into account in qualitative research. Therefore, it was ensured that potential participants do not feel pressured into taking part in the interviews and show a genuine interest in the topic. Furthermore, it is extremely important to avoid any leading questions during the interviews, i.e. questions that evoke the answer the researcher is hoping for to guarantee integrity.

Consequently, often it is beneficial for the researcher to repeat what was said in their own words and get confirmation if this is correct in order to make sure that nothing will be misinterpreted.

The guided interviews

The interviews took 30 to 40 minutes each and consisted of three parts. First, the participants were asked a few questions about their buying behavior and brand loyalty (regarding body care products) to establish their awareness of their own buying behavior. In the second part, the interviewees watched the first ad ('#LikeAGirl') and were asked a few basic questions regarding their first impression of the ad, followed by the same procedure for the second ad(s). This was done to get their initial unbiased reaction to each ad. The last part of the interview required comparison and contrasting between the two ads. The questions in this part dealt with the issue of empowerment in general and advertising in particular. The interview questions, as well as a sample full transcription of one of the interviews, can be found in the appendix 2 and 3.

4. The Analysis

Initially, the responses received during the interviews were different in many ways and not easily quantifiable. This goes to show that, while this is a topic that is of concern for these women, it is highly subjective. However, in the course of the transcripts' evaluation according to the arguments and theories discussed in the previous sections, common themes emerged. It became clear that, while the responses are colored by individual experiences (cf. also the criteria for choosing the respondents) and underlying social structures of different cultures, often the core messages are similar and their essence can be extracted for the purpose of discussion. Consequently, the following analysis is structured according to these themes. Additionally, a table with key quotes from the interviews can be found in Appendix 4.

4.1 Empowerment and advertising

In order to be able to fully understand the women's responses to the ads, their understanding of empowerment, as well as their attitude towards empowerment efforts being placed in advertisements, has to be established.

Among the responses, various definitions of empowerment can be discerned. However, the two ends of the spectrum clearly showcase what inspired these definitions: one is influenced by academia, the other by society and the media. Similar to the discussion in section 2.1, the academic definition includes elements of agency, choice, control, knowledge and equal opportunities. The other definition correlates to part of the criticism that was mentioned in section 2.2. For the respondents drawing dominantly from this definition, empowerment not only means to have the freedom to do what you want, it is also strongly tied to how women perceive themselves and the encouragement they can receive from someone else. It is more about feeling empowered, rather than actually having equal opportunities. Yet, as Anne points out, **"feeling empowered doesn't mean you have an impact"** (2018). While only the definitions of two women seem to bear elements of the academic definition, the others define the term according to these popular views criticized by many feminists.

However, they all agree that advertising is the right place to focus empowerment efforts on. The main reason for this is the potential of ads to educate people. One respondent puts it this way:

"All actions that put this society problem in front and in the minds of people [...] is good, [and] after a working day of 8-10 or 12 hours what do most people do? They sit in front of their television and look at ads." (Tereza).

Additionally, advertisements should not be the only place to focus empowerment efforts on. Yet, **"you need to start somewhere"** and ads provide an easy access to most people (Laurene). Even Anne, the respondent most critical of the trend, agrees with this notion, as a change of the whole system would need **"a much more radical approach but in the society we live in now, for mainstream, this is a good entry point or way to break the ice, to raise tiny awareness"** (Anne).

Concluding from these responses, it seems that in the eyes of some female consumers (although they show different levels of awareness and criticism of the issue) women are generally empowered through femvertising as it is a good place to start with certain empowerment efforts, i.e. making consumers aware of the issues / educating them. This ties in with the notion established in section 2.1: Advertising has the potential to contribute to the empowerment of women. Therefore, the following sections will investigate what about the chosen ads felt empowering to the interviewees to be able to get an idea of what an ideal 'empowering ad' should be like.

4.2 Reactions

The responses received regarding the chosen campaigns were based on initial reactions, as none of the women had seen any of the ads before. Additionally, they did not have the opportunity to prepare themselves for the questions. In general, '#LikeAGirl' was perceived to be more positive than the '#Stresstest' campaign which was met with conflicting feelings by some of the women (most like the first video but not the second). Regarding the empowerment of women, six themes emerge through the responses.

Relatability

The first theme is relatability, i.e. the characters being relatable to the audience who should, additionally, be able to relate to the themes processed in the ad. Both ads employ this tactic, however, they do so in a different way. '#LikeAGirl' is pulling at the audience's heartstrings in order to trigger emotions. The responses capture this perfectly, as most women's initial reactions include words such as **'touching'**, **'shocking'** and **'revealing'**. Anne is the only respondent who does not like the ad, it even makes her **'skin crawl'**. The '#Stresstest' campaign uses this theme as well but their approach is different. Most respondents can relate to the main character in the first ad, as they have been (or could imagine being) in similar situations. However, the second ad did not resonate with anybody on that level. This could be part of the reason why the second '#Stresstest' was liked the least. While this theme might not specifically be tied to the empowerment of women, it shows that emotive advertising can help connect to the audience.

Stereotyping

The second theme deals with challenging stereotypes and the status quo. While most women feel positively about the use of these elements in all ads, there was also some criticism regarding the execution. Katrin points out that the '#Stresstest' ads are merely **"mirroring situations that already exist whilst *Always* challenges status quo"**. Taking an opposing view, Anne argues that instead of challenging status quo, '#LikeAGirl' is **"tearing people down and then building them up again"**, while the '#Stresstest' campaign is reversing gender stereotypes in an **"easy going way"**.

Education

The third emerging theme is the education of the audience. This theme is arguably one of the most important as for the interviewees it is the driving force in the justification of the use of empowerment in advertising (see previous section). To most respondents it is also the main driver behind '#LikeAGirl' (instead of selling a product or brand image), with one even calling it a **"noble thing to do"** by the brand (Christine).

Agency

Theme number four concerns women's agency. This was mentioned, in different ways, specifically, regarding the '#Stresstest' campaign. Laurene points out that the female character **"takes the power"** and the ad is **"selling the super power of the person"** instead of the product. Dunja argues that this is an empowering ad because it shows women doing brave things which not everybody can do. Additionally, **"it's about being capable of doing the same job"** as a man without being defined by that comparison (Anne).

Peer support

Another important theme that is addressed in the responses is the encouragement from someone else, in this case, other women. Particularly, the apparent comradery between the two women in the first '#Stresstest' is appreciated by most women. Laurene feels that this part is **"really empowering"** as it shows **"someone else giving you just the little push that you need to just do it"**. With encouragement being an important factor in the definition of empowerment for many of the respondents, the ad is a good example of how this element can be employed in advertising.

Diversity

The last theme that emerged in the analysis is the diversity of the cast. It was mentioned by some that a diverse cast is more empowering to them. Consequently, they argue that as '#LikeAGirl' includes women, men and children, as well as their opinions, it is more empowering than the '#Stresstest' campaign, which only portrays two people. Dunja, for example, says she is **"affected and empowered [by a more diverse cast] because you get more ideas from different people and [the ad] becomes a more trusted one"**.

4.3 Facing criticism

As part of the interviews, the women were also asked about some of the criticism that has been aimed at the ads in order to analyze their reaction. The first criticism concerned the campaigns' taglines. While '#LikeAGirl' has been criticized for infantilizing women, only one respondent is offended by the tagline (even before mentioning the criticism). All others agree that this was used appropriately as the ad shows the problem and teaches the audience a lesson. Furthermore, some respondents say that there is no offense in using the term 'girl' to refer to women as this is just another term that is used to refer to females and there just the biological difference is referenced. Consequently, it can be argued that this last point seems to support the notion that femvertising is a type of approach that is still needed for the 'big mass', i.e. the mainstream audience, in order to raise awareness for and expose them to certain issues (cf. Anne), in this case the underlying stereotypes rooted in our society as discussed in section 2.1.

The criticism the '#Stresstest' campaign received discusses the fact that their taglines are putting the action that is necessary to further equality on women. None of the respondents agree with this statement. Rather, they like this aspect of the taglines as it gives women agency and courage. Instead of having the feeling women have to change themselves to reach equality (as was proposed in section 2.2), they take away a sense of power from such a message. As Laurene puts it,

> It's not good that women have to do something to close the wage gap but it is reality [...] and if you think that you don't need to do anything and things will come, it [sic] will not. So it's not a super positive thing but it shows that she can do it and it's more about the courage of the woman. She acts and I think that's pretty positive that you can at least try. (2018)

The second confrontation presented them with the fact that most femvertising ads usually promote products that somehow maintain women's bodies (e.g. body care and sports clothing) which goes against what empowerment is. However, the responses received are in favor of femvertising. One argument is that women, nowadays, still define themselves through their looks and, therefore, this is a good way to reach a big audience. Furthermore, Dunja argues that when using those products the feeling that women get as a result is encouraging them to act differently, i.e. they become more courageous. In general, the respondents seem to think that the value of getting these messages to the consumers is higher than what they pay for it (cf. consumerism) and, for the moment, they can live with that.

4.4 The ideal 'empowerment ad'

In the final question of the interview, the six women were asked to explain what their ideal 'empowerment ad' would be like, considering everything that was discussed before. The answers were very similar and it seems to be very clear for them what they expect from an ad that is empowering. One important feature of such an ad is, unsurprisingly, inclusivity. Empowering ads should include a diverse cast in which women (and men) can be themselves, i.e. they should not be defined by stereotypes and be able to do what they want.

Another aspect concerns the purpose of the ad. The ideal empowerment ad should not sell empowerment; it should sell the product. As Anne says, **"Don't make it about [empowerment], just do it!"**. By including a diverse cast and more stories of women, as well as removing gendered stereotypes, an ad can be empowering without pointing it out and exploiting this alleged empowerment at the same time. In addition to this point, ideally, such ads would be supported by CSR (Corporate Social Responsibility) initiatives. While it could be argued that

Nike, with their fitting slogan 'Just do it', have been incorporating the mentioned aspects in their ads for some time already, the brand did not come to the mind of any respondent when talking about the ideal 'empowerment ad'.

This could have to do with the third and last feature of such an ad: A focus on educating the audience. An empowering ad should not only educate consumers about social issues but also about the product's ingredients and benefits in a truthful way. This is seen as empowering because it informs consumers accurately and gives them the freedom to choose which product they would like to buy instead of tricking them into it. Furthermore, it can be considered a response to criticism of femvertising concerning the masking of true issues of inequality as the respondents long for ads which actually bring those issues to the forefront.

As none of the respondents referenced any existing adverts as examples to illustrate their points, it can be concluded that, in their point of view, the ideal 'empowerment ad' does not exist yet. However, they know exactly what such an ad should be made of.

5. Conclusion

In this project, the notion that two conflicting views regarding the issue of empowerment in advertising and the trend of 'femvertising' exist has been reaffirmed through the literature review and the analysis of the qualitative interviews. While, generally, many consumers and advertisers praise femvertising efforts as 'going in the right direction', feminist scholars are much more critical of the trend questioning the intentions behind it. They argue that femvertising blinds consumers; it masks true issues of inequality, avoids structural change and is a capitalist tool to enforce consumerism. It almost seems as if there exists a conflict between historic academic definitions of what should be done, i.e. what should empower women, versus what is actually happening in society nowadays, i.e. what actually empowers them in the present. The answer might well lie in-between these two opposing viewpoints.

Concluding this report, it is argued that advertising can contribute to (but not solely facilitate) the empowerment of women. As Cornwall suggests, changing the representations of women "is a form of social action that can have a powerful impact on women's sense of their own power" (Cornwall 2016: 354). This is underlined by the realization of the research project's aim and the objective of investigating attitudes of women towards femvertising: all women interviewed agree that advertising is a good place to focus empowerment efforts on due to the reach and potential impact it can have on consumers and the potential of raising awareness for certain issues. Therefore, advertising can be seen as one of the processes that produce shifts in consciousness which are needed to change the dominant discourse in society in order to enable true equality.

However, the content and execution of adverts is crucial. While the respondents feel that femvertising is a *good start* in the right direction, it does not seem to be considered the *ideal* approach for this social change by anyone. Although, at the moment, the value of sending an empowering message to consumers is higher than the negative effects such ads could potentially have, the respondents' ideal 'empowerment ad' appears to be quite different to a typical femvertising ad. An ad like this should not try to *sell* empowerment but rather *be* empowering and aim to sell a product or service instead. This kind of empowerment can be achieved through two main approaches. First, the ad should be inclusive and diverse, i.e. representative of all different kinds of people (of all genders), concerning not only physical representation but also the stories that are being told. Second, the ad should educate people about social issues, as well as the product's ingredients and benefits in a truthful way, as this allows consumers to have agency over their purchase choice. On top of this, companies should be consistent with the messages they send and follow up their ads with CSR initiatives in order to avoid the kind of criticism companies, such as Unilever, frequently receive (see section 2.2). Advertising practitioners can benefit from incorporating these insights into their strategies to genuinely contribute to the empowerment of women.

All in all, it was found that advertising has the capability of contributing to the empowerment of women. However, while femvertising can be considered a first step in the right direction, a more inclusive and humble approach (comprised of adverts which are empowering instead of trying to sell empowerment) is needed for the future. In accordance with Cornwall's approach to empowerment, this project can then be considered an important sign post on advertising's journey toward the unconditional equality of women and men. Especially, the insights from the qualitative interviews and the guide to the ideal 'empowerment ad' provides practitioners with some resources to take the next step.

Limitations

At this point, it must be mentioned that there are two important limitations in this work that need to be considered for future development. First, the size of the project should be underlined. It can point researchers and advertisers in the right direction, however, to investigate further it should be opened up for a bigger project with more resources in the future. In that regard, it could also be interesting to have a follow up meeting with the respondents after a few months to see if they started taking more notice of issues that were discussed or if they changed the way they look at ads. Furthermore, it might be beneficial to produce an advert according to the respondents' description of the ideal 'empowerment ad' and record and analyze their reactions in a similar way as it was done in this project in order to make a comparison possible.

The second limitation directly involves the research question and hypothesis. This project merely focuses on the empowerment and misrepresentation of women in advertising while there are other discriminated groups of people who receive the same treatment but not the same kind of attention, for example the LGBTQ+ community and people who are marginalized because of their ethnicity.

Including all of these groups in the report would have gone beyond the constraints of this research project. While it must be stressed that these groups should not be ignored, the researcher is not in accordance with Michael Roth's (CEO, Interpublic Group) approach of moving on to the next marginalized group now that women have received appropriate attention, a few changes have been accomplished and their case has been brought to the media (cf. Roth 2018). Instead, this project can be considered part of the foundation for a model of an all-inclusive advertising industry of the future.

Bibliography

AKESTAM, Nina, Sara ROSENGREN and Micael DAHLEN. 2017. 'Advertising "like a girl": Toward a better understanding of "femvertising" and its effects'. *Psychology & Marketing*, 34, 795-806.

ALWAYS. 2014. '#LikeAGirl'. Available at: https://www.youtube.com/watch?v=XjJQBjWYDTs [accessed 01 July 2018].

ANNE. 2018. Interview on Femvertising with L-M Koller [personal communication, 11 May 2018].

ASA. 2017. 'Depictions, perception and harm: A report on gender stereotypes in advertising'. Available at: https://www.asa.org.uk/asset/2DF6E028-9C47-4944-850D00DAC5ECB45B.C3A4D948-B739-4AE4-9F17CA2110264347/ [accessed 01 July 2018].

ASA and CAP. 2018. 'Gender Research'. Available at: https://www.asa.org.uk/genderresearch.html [accessed at 01 July 2018].

BEARD, Mary. 2017. *Women & Power: A Manifesto*. London: Profile Books LTD.

BERNAYS, Edward. 1965. *Biography of an Idea: Memoirs of Public Relations Counsel Edward L. Bernays*. New York: Simon and Schuster.

BLLOSHMI, Ana. 2013. 'Advertising in Post-Feminism: The Return of Sexism in Visual Culture?'. *Journal of Promotional Communications*, 1(1), 4-28.

CALKIN, Sydney. 2015. 'Post-Feminist Spectatorship and the Girl Effect: "Go ahead, really imagine her". *Third World Quarterly*, 36(4), 654-669.

CHRISTINE. 2018. Interview on Femvertising with L-M Koller [personal communication, 16 May 2018].

CORNWALL, Andrea. 2016. 'Women's Empowerment: What Works?'. *Journal of International Development* 28, 342-359.

D&AD. 2018. '9 Creative Campaigns That Celebrate Women'. *D&AD* [online]. Available at: https://www.dandad.org/en/d-ad-female-empowerment-award-winning-work/ [accessed 01 July 2018].

DE WAAL MALEFYT, Timothy and Maryann McCabe. 2016. 'Women's bodies, menstruation and marketing "protection: interpreting a paradox of gendered discourses in consumer practices and advertising campaigns'. *Consumption Markets & Culture*, 19(6), 555-575.

DOWSETT, Julie. E. 2010. 'Commodity Feminism and the Unilever Corporation: Or, How the Corporate Imagination Appropriates Feminism'. *Affinities: A Journal of Radical Theory, Culture, and Action*, 4(2), 9 - 16.

DUNJA. 2018. Interview on Femvertising with L-M Koller [personal communication, 28 May 2018].

EISEND, M. (2010). 'A meta-analysis of gender roles in

42

advertising'. *Journal of the Academy of Marketing Science*, 38(4), 418–440.

EISENSTEIN, Hester. 2017. 'Hegemonic Feminism, Neoliberalism and Womenomics: 'Empowerment' Instead of Liberation'. *Hegemonic Feminism*, 35-49.

EMGN. 2017. 'Nike has Empowered Women For 40 Years – Here Are Their Most Inspirational Campaigns!' *EMGN* [online]. Available at: http://emgn.com/entertainment/nike-has-empowered-women-for-40-years-here-are-their-most-inspirational-campaigns/ [accessed 01 July 2018].

FOOTE, Ami. 2017. '7 Powerful Ad Campaigns That Showcase Female Empowerment'. *L&T* [online]. Available at: http://landt.co/2017/02/female-empowerment-ad-campaigns/ [accessed 01 July 2018].

FORER, Laura. 2018. 'The Domination of Mobile Ads: Trends and Statistics [Infographic]'. *MarketingProfs* [online]. Available at: https://www.marketingprofs.com/chirp/2018/33818/the-domination-of-mobile-ads-trends-and-statistics-infographic [accessed 15 July 2018].

GILL, Rosalind and Shani ORGAD. 2017. 'Confidence Culture and the Remaking of Feminism'. *New Formations*, 16-34.

GOOGLE. 2016. 'YouTube ads leaderboard: International Women's Day Edition'. *Think with Google* [online]. Available at: https://www.thinkwithgoogle.com/advertising-channels/video/youtube-ads-leaderboard-international-womens-day-edition/ [accessed 01 July 2018].

GRIFFIN, Gabriele. 2017. *A Dictionary of Gender Studies* [online]. Oxford University Press. Available at: http://www.oxfordreference.com.ezproxy.falmouth.ac.uk/view/10.1093/acref/9780191834837.001.0001/acref-9780191834837 [accessed 01 July 2018].

HUIS, Marleoes Ac. Nina HANSEN, Sabine OTTEN and Robert LENSINK. 2017. 'A Three-Dimensional Model of Women's Empowerment: Implications in the Field of Microfinance and Future Directions'. *Frontiers in Psychology*, 8(1678).

KATRIN. 2018. Interview on Femvertising with L-M Koller [personal communication, 24 May 2018].

LAURENE. 2018. Interview on Femvertising with L-M Koller [personal communication, 25 May 2018].

MCROBBIE, Angela. 2009. The Aftermath of Feminism: Gender, Culture and Social Change (Culture, Representation and Identity Series). London: SAGE Publications Ltd.

METOOMOVEMENT. 2018. 'me too'. Available at: https://metoomvmt.org [accessed 01 July 2018].

NUDD, Tim. 2017. 'The 10 Most Viral Empowering Ads for Women on YouTube in 2016'. *AdWeek* [online]. Available at: https://www.adweek.com/creativity/the-10-most-viral-empowering-ads-for-women-on-youtube-in-2016/ [accessed 01 July 2018].

ONUOHA, Urey. 2016. 'Beyond Pink: Women in advertising'. *ANA Magazine (WARC)*.

ONEUPWEB. 2017. '9 Ads Empowering Women and Breaking Stereotypes'. *oneupweb* [online]. Available at: https://www.oneupweb.com/blog/9-ads-inspiring-women/ [accessed 01 July 2018].

PANKHURST, Helen. 2018. Interviewed by Lisa Smosarski during Advertising Week Europe 2018. Available at: http://europe.advertisingweek.com/replay/-shortlist-seminar-2018-03-20-1415 [accessed 01 July 2018].

PENNY, Laurie. 2017. *Bitch Doctrine: Essays for Dissenting Adults*. London: Bloomsbury Publishing.

ROTH, Michael. 2018. Interviewed by Farrah Storr during Advertising Week Europe 2018. Available at: http://europe.advertisingweek.com/schedule/-unstereotyped-michael-roth-2018-03-19-1015 [accessed 01 July 2018].

SAINI, Angela. 2017. *Inferior*. London: 4th Estate.

SECRET. 2016. '#StressTest'. Available at: https://www.youtube.com/watch?v=1Ug9uuCseq8 and https://www.youtube.com/watch?v=3Qkn1SCAANc [accessed 01 July 2018].

SKEY, Samantha. 2015. '#Femvertising'. *SheKnowsMedia* [online]. Available at: http://www.sheknowsmedia.com/attachments/204/iBlog_Magazine-SheKnows-FemvertisingFeature.pdf [accessed 01 July 2018].

STORY, Louise. 2007. 'Anywhere the Eye Can See, It's Likely to See an Ad'. *The New York Times* [online]. Available at:

https://www.nytimes.com/2007/01/15/business/media/15every
where.html [accessed 15 July 2018].

TEREZA. 2018. Interview on Femvertising with L-M Koller
[personal communication, 24 May 2018].

TIME'S UP. 2017. 'Time's Up'. Available at:
https://www.timesupnow.com [accessed 01 July 2018].

UNILEVER. 2017a. 'Announcing the Dove Real Beauty Pledge'.
Unilever [online]. Available at:
https://www.unilever.com/news/news-and-features/Feature-
article/2017/Announcing-the-Dove-Real-Beauty-Pledge.html
[accessed 01 July 2018].

UNILEVER. 2017b. 'Launch of Unstereotype Alliance set to
eradicate outdated stereotypes in advertising'. *Unilever* [online].
Available at: https://www.unilever.com/news/Press-
releases/2017/launch-of-unstereotype-alliance-set-to-eradicate-
outdated-stereotypes-in-advertising.html [accessed 01 July
2018].

USBORNE, Simon. 2016. 'Mad Men and invisible women: how
the advertising industry failed to move on'. *The Guardian*, 25
June 2016, 36.

ZEISLER, Andi. 2016. *We Were Feminists Once: From Riot Grrrl to
CoverGirl®, the Buying and Selling of a Political Movement*. USA:
PublicAffairs.

Appendix 1: Consent Form

Participant Consent Form

Full title of project: Can ads genuinely facilitate the empowerment of women?

Name, position and contact details of researcher:

Lisa-Marie Koller, BA, Student (LK195283@falmouth.ac.uk, +436603555477)

Name, position and contact details of supervisor:

Amber Burton, Course Leader (amber.burton@falmouth.ac.uk)

To be completed by the participant:	
I confirm that I have read and understood the participant information sheet for the above research project and have had the opportunity to ask questions.	
I understand and give my permission that this interview will be audio recorded and possibly be transcribed so as to prove the validity of the quotes used by the researcher.	
I understand that my participation is voluntary and that I am free to withdraw at any time, without giving reason and without there being any negative consequences. In addition, should I not wish to answer any particular question(s), I am free to decline.	
I give permission for members of the research team to have access to my anonymized responses. I understand that my name will not be linked with the research materials, and I will not be identified or identifiable in the report or reports that result from the research. There will be no use of recognizable audio or visual materials in conferences and presentations.	
I agree to take part in the above research project.	

Name of Participant   Date   Signature

Name of Researcher   Date   Signature

Once this has been signed by all parties the participant should receive a copy of the signed and dated participant consent form, the participant information sheet and any other written information provided to the participants. A copy of the signed and dated consent form should be kept with the project's main documents which must be kept in a secure location.

Appendix 2: Interview Questions

Interview Questions

Part X:
Very briefly, please state your name, age, profession and where you come from.

- Are you loyal to brands (re body care) or do you change easily?
- Do you use the same brands (re body care) your mother used?
- What would encourage you to switch to a different brand in the body care sector?

Part 1:
The Always ad was shown first and then the following questions were asked, followed by the Secret ad and the same questions:

- What did you think about the ad (briefly)? (start off with this to get the first impression without them thinking too much about specific topics)

- Would you be more willing or less willing to buy the brand's products after seeing the ad? Would you even consider switching your brand? And why?
- Were you aware of what kind of product this is an ad for while watching?

Part 2:
After Part 1, this part continues with questions that might require comparison or contrasting between the two ads:

- What is empowerment for you?
- Do you think the ads I just showed you are empowering? All or just one? Why?
- What do you think about the taglines? (i.e. calling all women "girls" or putting the action necessary to further equality to the women by stating "she does her part in closing the wage gap")
- A lot of ads that claim to empower women (like the ones I just showed you) are for products or services that are there to help "maintain" women's bodies (c.f. also Dove, Sports England, Nike, Rimmel). Do you think this is the right place to focus empowerment efforts on? Or even completely wrong? Do you think it's objectifying women? Please explain why.
- What would an ad that is empowering look like for you?

Appendix 3: Interview Transcript

Sample full transcription of one interview

Interview on Femvertising with Katrin* (participant) and L-M Koller (interviewer),
24 May 2018

I = Interviewer
P = Participant

I: Can you please state your name, your profession, your age and where you come from.

P: My name is Katrin*, I'm 48 years old and I'm the global key account manager for one of our major food accounts. I'm based in Vienna, Austria. And nationality wise: I'm German.

I: Thank you. So, a few short questions before we start with the ads. The first one is: Are you loyal to brands? Specifically, body care brands, or do you change easily?

P: I change very easily.

I: Why do you change? What would encourage you to change a brand?

P: I don't have a particular strong emotion or product benefit relationship to any of my body care brands. With one exception, maybe. So, I take whatever looks appealing the day I need to refresh my products.

I: Ok. What is the exception?

P: Hygiene products.

I: So there you stick to the same -

P: I stick to the same brand all the time, yeah.

I: Ok. Do you use the same brands, body care brands or maybe specifically hygiene, that your mother used?

P: No.

I: Is there a specific reason?

P: Because they are not available. I´m coming from the eastern part of Germany. So they were just not available back then.

I: And the reason you stick to this brand is content wise or is it the brand itself? Is it ingredients or ...?

P: It is my knowledge about alternatives, much rather. It´s availability of the product and satisfaction with the product.

I: Ok. And the other products, that are body care, but not this specific product - What would encourage you to switch there? Would it be brand image, would it be an ad, would it be something you see and you think "Ah, this looks nice" or is it ingredients?

P: If I consider a change or if I would move to making a deliberate decision on this, it would be the ingredients.

I: Ok. Thank you! So, then we can move on to the first ad.

[watching Always '#LikeAGirl']

Very briefly: First reactions. What did you think about the ad?

P: I find it very touching. I previously encountered the type of discussion with the customer I'm looking after in the area of skin care. And it's something that I can relate to. Because I observed this, I never quite, I never quite had it, you know, being shown straight to your face. I really liked the way it is expressed. I like the way the ad is scripted ... No, it's a very nice, a very touching ad. Actually, challenging stereotypes and status quo. So, that's the type of ads I would like.

I: Ok. So, after seeing this ad, would you be more or less willing to buy the brands product?

P: More.

I: More? Ok.

P: If I wouldn't already buy it, I would definitely be.

I: And where you aware of what kind of product this is an ad for while watching?

P: Yes, because I know the brand.

I: Ok. So, you recognized the brand in the ad?

P: Yeah.

I: *Thank you! So, then we can watch the second ad(s).*

[watching both Secret '#StressTest' ads]

So, again briefly: What did you think about the ad or the ads?

P: Um... I like the ... You said they run for the same campaign, right?

I: *Yes. So, they had a number of different stress tests in the same campaign.*

P: I like one better than the other. I like the first one better than the, than the second one. Compared to the first ad you have shared, I liked these less.

I: *Why?*

P: Because it has less of a purpose. It's more ..., it's more stereotype.

I: *M-h-m ... Ok, so, if you not, if you don't compare it to the Always one, do you have any more thoughts on the ads? ... So, you liked the first one better? Why?*

P: I thought there was more of a ... of a story to tell and there was a ... comradery between the women, um, which, you know, the older one supporting the younger one for um, going for what she thinks was right. Whilst, the second one, umm, umm, I don't know ... felt ... I don't see much of a strong story here.

I: Ok. Thank you! Then, would you be more or less willing to buy the brands products after seeing the ads?

P: Umm, ... is there something, I´m probably not .... I´m indifferent. I wouldn´t buy it because of the ads.

I: Ok. And, were you aware of what kind of product this is an ad for while watching?

P: I can only guess. I guess it´s like a deodorant or something.

I: Yeah. But only at the end you saw this? Or during the whole ad you already thought this is a deodorant?

P: Umm, mmm ... I don´t know when I noticed. ... I couldn´t say when I thought that this is about ...

I: But before you saw the products? Or you can´t say?

P: ... Hmm, well I guess it was, because when you're anxious ... I guessed what it was and when I saw the product it confirmed what I thought it was.

I: Ok. So, now the second part. I'm going to ask you some questions, that might require some kind of comparison or contrasting between the ads and this is then also about the empowerment of women through ads. So, the first one is still general - What is empowerment for you? So, really for you. What do you think is empowerment?

P: ... Empowerment for me has various different dimensions ... of which one is to have the freedom to operate and the freedom to act. It has, is also about, um, basically knowing what to do. So it has an element of knowledge being ... yeah being knowledgeable and having the ability and the confidence to be able to do things.

I: Ok. So, with this in mind, do you think the ads that I just showed you are empowering? If all of them yes, why? But if just one, also why?

P: This is where I see a big difference between the first ad you shared and the other two. Although they all kind seem to have, um, women in .... they all seem to be women centric, one is, um, really ... getting to underline courses, which was the first one rather than the other two using stereotype situations. Which, of course they exist, but they are just, they are just mirroring a situation that we know is existing whilst the first ad is challenging status quo. In terms what is more empowering clearly to me, this is the first one.

I: So, but do you think the other two are empowering as well or just the first one?

P: Umm ... um ... empowerment also has a bit to do with encouragement and there was an element in the ... in the first one of the second series, when the older lady popped up, then there was this element of encouragement, which is not exactly the same thing. Umm ... so I don´t know whether you are particularly keen on defining the term empowerment. I didn´t find it particularly empowering. I found it encouraging, but not empowering.

I: Ok. And, you said that the first one, the Always ad, kind of challenges status quo and the others are mirroring stereotypical situations. But, they are also turning them around. Do you still think this is just mirroring them? Because the Always one also says, first, "Like a girl", but then they say "but we can do it differently". The other two, the Secret ads, they also show something ---

P: Exactly. So, it is ... They are just turning it around and trying to make a male situation look like a female. Because even if you are a young male and you think you have done a great job and you have a great achievement, you could still end up in front of a mirror of a bathroom wondering how to bring it across. The fact that you are a woman doesn't make it any different to me. It's a ... It assumes ... It's kind of false ... false empowerment, if you want. Or false, ummm, I don't know how to express that ... Particularly the last one is ... If you wanna purpose to your partner, I guess, I can only guess it's equally exiting, whether you are a man or whether you are a woman. And if you have an idiot like this guy in front of yourself, you should really think twice whether you wanna do it. So, I don't know if this was meant to be comical. It's something, the later one doesn't speak to me at all, umm, and it ... And I'm also not a great fan of saying that a woman necessarily have to do all the same things the same way that men do. So, I still hope that in 200 years from now you will still have a man proposing to a woman and it's not a sign of ... equal rights that ... You know ... I still hope that there would be ... That we can live, umm, some, I don't know, tradition. That's what it is. Of reversing everything, and having woman being able to do everything a man does, I don't think is the answer to empowerment.

I: Ok. Thank you! Then, the next one is about the tag line. So, the first one is "Like a girl", then the others are about doing something to further the empowerment. So, this one says "at three o'clock Lucy does her part ... to close the wage gap". This one is also very similar. It's "Claire's act of romance flips the script on centuries old tradition".

P: And this is what I hate.

I: The last tag line?

P: The last one I really don't like. Just ... I don't know ... It's a very personal thing. The other one on closing the wage, on closing the wage gap, umm, it actually ... I have to say I'm only reading this tag like now. Um, ... it does have a kind of purpose. But the way the story is told, I don't find very ... addressing the heart of what she is trying to do.

I: Ok. And, they are saying that to further equality basically she has to do her part. Um, do you agree with this that they are saying this or did you see it differently? ... Do you think there is a problem with that? That she has to do something to close the wage gap?

P: Ummm ... Umm, no, I don't have a problem with this.

I: And the "Like a girl"? So, with this one they say women are girls. Do you have a problem with this? Do you think this is ok? Did you have any thoughts on this?

P: This is a very particular case. Because there is a very similar series of adverts in Austria around 'BIPA', which I actually hated.

The execution of this I think is insulting to be honest. Whilst, the execution here, I liked. And I have a very different emotional connection to this one than I have to the 'BIPA' one, although they say the same thing. So, it's not only about the message, it's also about how you tell the story, which I really, the execution, I really like in this one.

I: Can you say a bit more about why?

P: Ummm, it is, um … why do I like this more … Um, because it teaches me a lesson. I think it teaches me a lesson, which is that, um, you know you raise your children and they, the girls they think they are equally strong up until they enter into teenage. And I wasn't … I wasn't that aware that … You kind of know, but here you have mirror … It's a strong message, where I think I have a role to play. So, I … I guess, a lesson that I take for myself, it's something I can relate to, that I would carry back to how I act. So, there is a kind of a purpose, a deeper sense. Whilst, for the one, you know, which uses the same tag line, the 'BIPA' one, I … To me it's not a message to want to behave like a girl for the rest of your life. It's not what I aspire to, I don't think it's right. But here it is … it is just a deeper meaning.

I: And also turning around this phrase maybe? To mean something more positive? Is it also an aspect?

P: Ummm, to me it never was really, it was never a negative term. But, I kind of now, get the point of what it actually means maybe to some people. Umm, … You know, I'm coming from a generation, actually also from a country where there was, where female rights or female work force, the strength of women and society and work places was common place. It's actually funny for

58

me to see that that is not necessarily the case in all of the developed societies. I mean I know by now, but I'm coming from a very different background and this girlish, um, let's be honest, there is also some kind of truth in this. You know, the way how young women act at times, ummm, ... were correctly mirrored. So there's ... It's not only a false assumption, it's there is also some truth in this. So, umm, to challenge this, yeah, I think I like the idea.

I: Ok. Thank you! So, one more, that is maybe a bit longer, and then a short one and then we are done. So, the next one is about that, um, a lot of ads and also the ones that you just saw but also a lot more, claim to empower women. But they are ads for products or services that help to maintain women's' bodies. For example, the ones you saw, but also Dove,or there is Sports England, there is Nike, Rimmel ... So, sports, clothing, make up, other body care, hygiene ... So, do you think this is the right place to focus the empowerment efforts on ... or completely wrong? Or do you even think it's maybe objectifying women, because it's all about maintaining their bodies? And in this way, encouraging empowerment?

P: Oh Jesus, this is a very deep psychological question. Ummm, ... I think ... well one ... Empowerment is not an abstract thing by any means. It's something which is very concrete and you feel it the most in things that affect you on a very regular basis. You know, it's no point on discussing empowerment on a political topic or highly intellectual, if you are never exposed to that, if you never come in contact with this, if ... you are not interested. So, the first step to empowerment is to go to where people have contact with, um, products, with the way of living, with ... So, the fact that it does, it's done with consumer goods and things that are part of your day to day life is very natural and makes perfect sense to me. ... Umm, now, what I do like, and here I´m closing the loop again, so you said like there are brands that, um, put this, um, into the focus and you mentioned one around Dove, which they have actually had a campaign many years back where they said "unstereotype" and they have shown women of all sizes, color, whatever ... Umm, It, I mean where else do you wanna show and, um, ... highlight of where the challenges are in society. Now, you are right with the flip sight of that coin, which is that, because this is such a massive industry you always have the impression, that if you don´t buy the next anti-wrinkle crème you're gonna be the biggest loser. So, I think we are looking at the same coin from, um, two different sides. But, it is, if it is about empowerment of women, um, wanting to look good is not a new phenomenon. It´s something that is, you know, I guess it´s not only true by the way for women, it´s also true for men. They had other means and the beauty industry discovers that men are an equally good source of an income. So, it´s not a female phenomenon. So, um, ... what I would make the distinction thought is the difference between what is this empowerment wash so similar to, like, the green wash and more, more, I don´t know, deeper ... deeper challenge. And this was a very well shown in the ads here. You know, there are some things here whether, I don´t know, facial crèmes or whatever else you have ... I don´t give a damn shit. Excuse my language, but ... um, to have a healthy skin definitely is a desirable thing, whether I have a wrinkle more or less, I don´t care. And this is a very fine, a very fine .... fine line.

I: Ok. Just to make sure, that we didn´t skip anything - about the objectification of women through these kind of ads - You don´t think it´s objectifying women? If I got that right.

P: For those particular ones you have shown, it doesn't.

I: And in general?

P: In general there are many around that still do, yeah.

I: But those you say --

P: But those, the three ones we have looked at, no.

I: Ok. So, the last question is of everything that we just talked about. What would an ad that is empowering look like for you? So, would it be something like what you saw or would it be something completely different? Or a mix or what would it be like? ... Empowering to women.

P: ... So, back to the original question of what empowerment means, if the ad gives me some kind of education, um, ... if it does give me some kind of encouragement to ... to do what I really do well or, you know, be true to myself or even encourage to go above and beyond, um, ... that definitely or yeah. It educates, it challenges thinking, um, ... and leaves me choice and freedom, then this would be ... that would be an empowering one.

I: Choice and freedom in which regard? Buying the products or more in the empowerment ---

P: Umm —

I: -- If you want to act upon it? Or what kind of choice and freedom?

P: Umm, ... well this is a bit of an ... It almost goes to what, um, advertisement should be. At the end of the day, um, empowerment is a big promise for a fast moving consumer good, right? So, what I would expect that to do is to also ... be real and not over-promise. So, I ... if I say the freedom of choice I want the message to be true. I think that's what it is. Take the example of the deodorant. Um ... The deodorant whatever other, you know, secondary agenda they have, it should still fulfill the purpose, which is, you know, preventing me from sweating or smelling bad. It's still needs to ... it needs to still deliver the basic, um, product, the basic product benefits. It can't ... I'm not gonna safe the world with a ... with a product. So there needs to be, um, also a reality check or a sense of ... reality. So, things are not overpromised, they are not other things hidden by, you know like, I don't know, by bad material that's being in a deodorant that are not good for me. On one hand, you know, I want to be empowered, on the other hand I'm sneaking things into my body that shouldn't be there. So, it's probably product truths and product transparency and, um, ... and I would expect that companies that are producing this are living the philosophy that they showcase in their ads in their own company.

I: Ok. Thank you! Do you have anything that is related to this that I didn't ask, that you want to say?

P: Ummm, No, I think you have covered quite a comprehensive view on the topic. So, good look! It's a very interesting subject.

I: Thank you!

*This is not the participants real name. The name was changed due to confidentiality reasons.

Appendix 4: Key Quotes from Interviews

	Anne	Christine	Dunja	Katrin	Laurene	Tereza
Empowerment	- [Empowerment is] making people believe they can actually do what they want and guarantee systems where this is possible, that everyone has equal opportunities and have a choice and feel like they are in control (as far as possible) of their life and choices. - Feeling empowered doesn't mean you have an impact.	[Empowerment is] feeling stronger or more confident, having more responsibility.	[Empowerment is:] I have to feel that I am free.	There is no point in discussing empowerment on a political or highly intellectual [level] if you never come in contact with this, if you are not interested. The first step is to go to where the people have contact with products, the way of living.	Empowerment is the fact that you can do everything that you want to do […]. Maybe something […] you think for whatever reason, maybe because you're a woman, or too young, it's not your country, you're maybe not the best to do it – and maybe you have someone that tells you but you can do it, encourage you, empower you actually.	For women it's more difficult than for men to do what they want and how they perceive themselves.

Empowerment in Advertising (specifically regarding body care products)	- A much more radical approach [is needed] but in the society we live in now, for mainstream, this is a good entry point or way to break the ice, to raise tiny awareness. - [The ideal empowerment ad:] Don't make it about it [empowerment], just do it, be inclusive.	Women shouldn't feel empowered by the products themselves. [...] The ads shouldn't be there to empower women just to sell the products but to raise awareness for women in general.	Women want to take care of their bodies, it's all about their bodies, but it's also a feeling. It's not only about using something and seeing the results, the result is also a feeling. For me the more important thing is the feeling, it's empowering.	There is a difference between 'empowerment-wash' similar to the 'green-wash' and a more deeper challenge very well shown in the ads.	You need to start somewhere. [...] So if you can have some tools that help you go further and be more empowered and if it's a question of you feel better because you look more beautiful today or you don't sweat when you go to your boss then why not?	- All actions that put this society problem in front and in the minds of people [...] is good, [and] after a working day of 8-10 or 12 hours what do most people do? They sit in front of their television and look at ads. - [The ideal empowerment ad:] just does it [empowerment] and doesn't get my attention in that way.

Relatability					
- There is much more variation in identifying like a girl [than shown in the ad]. - [The Secret ad shows] a much more realistic setting, something that could happen in real life, doesn't make such a big deal out of it.	In the first [Secret] ad I feel like I can connect with the girl, i've been in a lot of situations in which I felt like her.	[Secret] I didn't like it because if this is an ad I want a relationship [with the characters or the brand].	[Always] I like the ad, I find it very touching.	[Always] I was shocked at the beginning and then I understood it. I think it's pretty well done.	The first [Secret ad] was funny. Everyone knows how these situations are when you need to prepare for something what you want to say to a boss or customer.

Stereotyping				
	- By putting this out there its suggesting that being like a girl is a bad thing and then trying to change it but why do you have to insist its like that first? - Both [campaigns] are about the same topic – changing the rules, what is a woman supposed to do, what not – but very differently. [In the Secret ad] there is a reversal of gender stereotypes in an easy going way, not super exaggerated.	I got the impression that if everybody is equal it shouldn't be like this, to say being like a girl, there is a very big labelling here. Like people want to put a label on top of people's gender. It is not a harsh ad, a very nice way of saying that we are not different.	Always is really getting to underline causes rather than the other two using stereotype situations which of course exist but are just mirroring situations [...] whilst Always challenges status quo [which makes Always more empowering].	- [The second Secret ad is disturbing because] it still appears like it's something stereotypical that a man has to ask a woman, that it's new that a woman asks a man but its already something normal. - I think a normal ad for me would be were not this typical silly behavior of women would be shown but just a normal ad and where women can be just people. It's that they are female or men but they are not identified by their behavior or stereotypes.

Education					
[An ad is] a good way to put the message out there but it's still to sell a product – everything we see changes the way we think, [therefore an ad] can build awareness.	- It's noble of the brand, a good thing to talk about those kind of things, to make people think about what doing something like a girl really means. - [Women] should just look at the message and that would empower them because maybe they can learn something new or it can open their eyes in some kind of way without having the product linked to it.	[The ideal empowerment ad] should explain what it includes and how [the hair] is straight, I need more info. [This is empowering] because I'm interested to have details about the product and then you have the freedom to choose which product you want.	- [Always] The execution I really like in this one because it teaches me a lesson [...] – here you have a mirror and it's a strong message where I have a role to play. - [The ideal empowerment ad] gives me some kind of education [...] challenges thinking and leaves me choice and freedom.		[Always] I like it because it makes us aware that this is a huge problem and even women who don't seem stupid in this clip assume that like girl is a bad thing.

Agency				
- [The Secret ad] is also in a way about comparing yourself to a man but you're not defined by the comparison with a man, it's about being capable of doing the same job.		- [The Secret ads] are also empowering but in a different way. These two women are doing brave things which not all people can do and this affected me.	- [Secret] They don't sell the super power of the product but more the super power of the person that wears it. - [Secret – 2nd ad] She takes the power so somehow its empowering. - [Secret taglines] put the woman character and her action first, so the action is defining these women. It's not good that women have to do something to close the wage gap but it is reality [...] and if you think that you don't need to do anything and things will come, it [sic] will not. So it's not a super positive thing but it shows that she can do it and it's more about the courage of the woman. She acts and i think that's pretty positive that you can at least try.	- [Secret taglines] I like the last ones because we should close all these centuries old traditions where only the men can do it and a woman has to wait until a man acts and we're just admiring. I like them. We shouldn't wait and i thin society should be more aware of that. [...] it has to get normal, then also other stuff will get normal in society, like the salary.

Peer Support				
[Secret] I like the woman-on-woman empowerment in the first one.	[The Secret ads] are empowering because they showed us that we shouldn't be afraid of doing this and we can do them even though we are nervous about them or they are things that usually men do, we are able to do them just as well.	[The Always ad is empowering] because it makes me feel like I can do what I want and don't think about the other's opinion, be yourself, have your own way.	[Secret] There was an element of encouragement in the first one with the older lady popping up.	[Secret] The first one with the woman in the toilet with the other woman is what I was talking about, someone else giving you just the little push that you need to just do it and just jump. That part is really empowering.

Diversity			
	[Always] There are only two people in the ad – this is affective for me because if you hear something from different people its also important, that's why I'm affected and empowered – because you get more ideas from different people and it becomes more trusted.		[About the ideal empowerment ad] I would remove this gender story because that's already putting you down from one step. [...] include men in these stories so that you have an equal situation.

Printed in Poland
by Amazon Fulfillment
Poland Sp. z o.o., Wrocław